Compilation copyright © 1990 by Dick Bruna Books, Inc.
Illustrations Dick Bruna, copyright © Mercis bv, 1964, 1967, 1968, 1969, 1972, 1973,
1979, 1982, 1986

Created and manufactured by Dick Bruna Books, Inc., by arrangement with
Ottenheimer Publishers, Inc. Illustrations by Dick Bruna.
No part of this book may be reproduced in any form without written permission from
the publisher.

First published in Great Britain in 1990 by William Collins Sons & Co Ltd,
8 Grafton Street, London W1X 3LA

A CIP catalogue record for this book is available from the British Library

0 00 184578 0

Printed in Italy

I know my numbers

Dick Bruna

COLLINS

=

1

one

=

2

two

= **3**

three

=

4

four

=

5

five

=

6

six

=

7

seven

= **8**

eight

=

9

nine

= **10**

ten

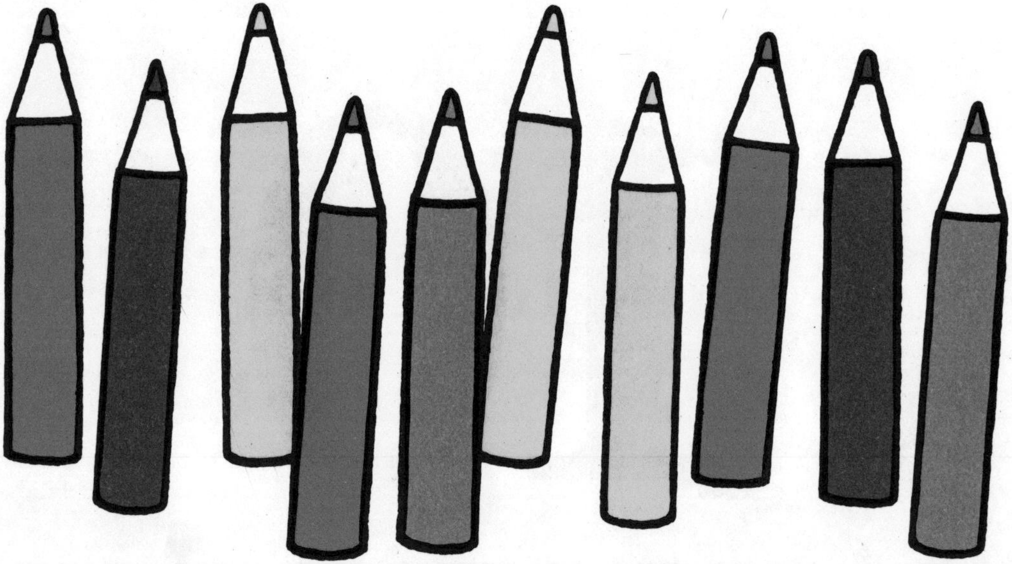

How many pencils?

How many flowers?